Thank you to my Aunt Eileen for instilling in me almost every day for the past 2 years that I can do anything I want and will be HUGELY SUCCESSFUL.

Thank you to my children and grandchildren for being my WHY in everything I do.

Thank you to my parents for giving me the gift to write and create.

Thank you to Teresa, Kelsi and Taylor for always being game to have anything read, anywhere, anytime.

Thank you to Taylor for coming up with the wonderful title to the book.

And a huge thankyou to my amazing illustrator! Justena – You were a dream to work with! Thank you!

And to my Doug,

thank you for our fur babies and for showing me

love comes softly.

Pawflection

Author: Traci Kay Davis
Illustrator: Justena Amiotte

Once upon a time, there was a puppy who said to her mommy,

"Mommy, I look like a bunny. I hop like a bunny and I am soft like a bunny."

"Am I a bunny?"

Mommy said, "Charlie girl, you look like a bunny, you hop like a bunny and you are soft like a bunny, but you are a Lachon puppy. You are also my baby and I love you very, very much."

The next day, Charlie's brother Bosco, said to their mommy,

"Mommy, I run like a greyhound. I race like a greyhound and my ears look like a greyhound."

"Am I a greyhound?"

Their mommy said, "Bosco, you run like a greyhound, you race like a greyhound, and your ears look like a greyhound, but you are a Jack Russell/Lachon puppy. You are also my baby and I love you very, very much!"

The next day, Charlie and Bosco's brother, Jack said to their mommy,

"Mommy, I smile like a tiger. I hunt like a tiger and I pounce like a tiger."

"Am I a tiger?"

Their mommy said, "Jack, you smile like a tiger. You hunt like a tiger and you pounce like a tiger, but you are a Jack Russel puppy. You are also my baby and I love you very, very much."

The next day, Charlie, Bosco and Jack's brother, Woody said to their mommy,

"Mommy, I look like a panther. I am quiet like a panther and I am brave like a panther."

"Am I a panther?"

Their mommy said, "Woody, you look like a panther. You are quiet like a panther and brave like a panther, but you are a black lab puppy. You are also my baby and I love you very, very much."

The next day Charlie, Bosco, Jack and Woody's sister Reese, said to their mommy,

"Mommy, I hunt like a bear. I growl like a bear and my nickname is Baby Bear."

"Am I a bear?"

Their mommy said, "Reese, you hunt like a bear. You growl like a bear and your nickname is Baby Bear, but you are a Yorkie puppy. You are also my baby and I love you very, very, much!"

The next day Charlie, Bosco, Jack, Woody and Reese's brother, Spud, said to their mommy, "Mommy, when you rub my belly, I look like a kangaroo. I jump like a kangaroo and can hear like a kangaroo."

"Am I a kangaroo?"

Their mommy said, "Spud, you look like a kangaroo. You jump like a kangaroo and hear like a kangaroo, but you are a yellow lab puppy. You are also my baby and I love you very, very much!"

One night while sitting around the fireplace, the puppies said to their mommy,
"Mommy, you call us your babies. You snuggle with us like we are your babies. You play with us like we are your babies. You sing, dance, and talk to us like we are your babies."

"Are we your babies?"

Mommy looked at each one of the puppies as she said their name, "Charlie, Bosco, Jack, Woody, Reese, and Spud, you have so many things in common with other babies, but these same things are also unique to you and who you are. You bring me smiles, joy, snuggles and love every day. You are my puppies and YES, you are my babies and I love you very, very much."

Jack – Our journey started with you. Thank you for being the best fur baby we could ask for!
Jack; 2003-2014

Here are photos of the puppies this book was based on. Our new Jack, Spud and Woody are the best of friends. All 3 of them work very hard at the lodge with their daddy.

Charlie Girl, Reese and Bosco are our other babies. We hope to bring many more adventures to our readers about the Paw Crew at Dakota Wild Wings Lodge.

Pickle ball puppy

Traci Kay Davis – Author
www.tracikaydavis.com

Pawflections is my first children's book. I am looking forward to bringing more stories to the readers about the Paw Crew at Dakota Wild Wings.

I have been a writer my whole life. I have loved to read ever since being a young child. My mother worked for our community newspaper and my dad is a natural story-teller. I was active in the school newspaper and yearbook staff. I submitted articles to our local newspaper while in high school. I had a type-writer and I loved the sound of the "click click" of the keys and the grind of the roller when you slid it back. I look at writing as a unique way to love, cry, rage and fight. It gives us power. It allows us to get lost in our imagination or to get lost in the facts. You will find both within my website.
Traci Kay Davis is from the prairies of the Dakotas. She grew up in the foothills of South Dakota, eventually dividing her time time between her homes in the City of Mitchell, home to the World's Only Corn Palace and Miller, SD, home of Dakota Wild Wings Hunting Lodge.

Justena Amiotte is a children's book illustrator specializing in painting animals and scenery. By growing up in the Badlands of South Dakota, it has given her a large appreciation for nature and its creatures. She strives to show the beauty and personality of them in each illustration. She has been illustrating for private clients for four years and is constantly striving to improve the quality of her work by taking online classes through Brainstorm Burbank, CA. Justena will be a graduate of Dakota Wesleyan University in 2022, with a major in Digital Media and Design and a minor in Entrepreneurial Leadership. You can reach Justena through her email: ajustena@yahoo.com